1984

To Mom and Dad

Happy Anniversary!

Love always,
Carolyn and Lee

COLORADO
AND THE ROCKIES

A PICTURE BOOK TO REMEMBER HER BY

Designed by
DAVID GIBBON

Produced by
TED SMART

CRESCENT

INTRODUCTION

The discovery of a Paleo-Indian camp at Lindenmeier Ranch in Eastern Colorado, in the 1930's, gave a clear picture of life in that part of the state shortly after 9000 BC. At that time the mammoth had begun to die off and bands of Indians probably gathered at the site for communal hunts of bison, antelope and deer. Once caught, these animals were utilised for food and clothing and also tools, examples of which were found amongst the twenty thousand or more artefacts excavated at the ranch.

Colorado's early history continues with another group of people called the Anasazi, who inhabited various parts of the South West, including what is now Mesa Verde National Park. Here can be seen a wealth of Anasazi ruins, a labyrinth of stone and mortar dwellings called pueblos. They were built either on the mesa top, well hidden by dense vegetation, or nestling in the canyon cliffs below. The best known pueblos are named Cliff Palace, Balcony House and Spruce Tree House and have been carefully preserved as a fascinating outdoor museum, an insight into life in AD 400–1300. By 1400 the Anasazi had moved away from this region and gradually tribes of Red Indians such as the Navajo took their place.

In 1541, the Spaniard Coronado led an expedition from Mexico across South East Colorado in search of the legendary Quivera and its Seven Cities of Cibola, whose streets were reputedly paved with gold. Their quest was fruitless and so, apart from a few French fur trappers who arrived about 1700, Colorado remained one of the least developed parts of America. The main reason for this was that, although migration from East to West had begun, the main wagon trails, like the Santa Fe and the Oregon trails, largely bypassed mountainous Colorado. However, in 1858 a Georgia prospector named Green Russell, who was married to a Cherokee Indian, found a small amount of gold on the banks of Cherry Creek where Denver, Colorado's capital, now stands. The gold-diggers flooded in. Many of these immigrants in fact found nothing or just a little of the irresistible mineral, but the following year richer deposits were discovered and the twin towns of Central City and Blackhawk came into existence and other strikes followed.

A certain William Hepburn Russell, a man of great foresight, saw a chance to make a fortune during these Gold Rush days, by opening a stagecoach line to Denver. He purchased a large number of Concord stagecoaches but before very long his venture collapsed. He therefore decided to inaugurate a fast mail service from the Missouri River to California – the Pony Express. To find suitable riders, Russell advertised in several newspapers "Wanted – young, skinny, wiry fellows not over 18. Must be expert riders willing to risk death daily. Orphans preferred". Of the numerous applicants he chose 80, one of whom was a fifteen year old boy named William Frederick Cody, who would be known in later years as Buffalo Bill. Although he only remained with the Pony Express from 1860–1861 he was to complete one of the longest rides on record. He fought for a time with the 7th Kansas Cavalry in the Civil War and later scouted for the 16th US Cavalry on the plains in several campaigns against the Indians. In addition he made a contract in 1867 with the Kansas Pacific Railroad Company to supply buffalo meat to its labourers. In eighteen months he is said to have killed 4,000 beasts. From 1883 he organized a Wild West Show with which he toured extensively in the United States and Canada. Sioux Chief Sitting Bull and Annie Oakley were amongst its stars. Cody eventually died in Denver in 1917 and is buried on top of Lookout Mountain.

Returning to the mid 19th century, another group of people, besides the gold prospectors, entered Colorado. They were American fur hunters who both traded worthless merchandise to the Indians for profitable pelts, and trapped animals themselves. At that time beaver fur was fetching a high price for fashionable hats and the Colorado Rockies were the source of many fine beaver streams. However, the trappers had to wade for miles in icy waters so as not to leave a scent and their best lure was a bundle of twigs smeared with a beaver's musk gland. Their way of life was hard and in order to survive the harsh mountain conditions they learned the ways of the Red Indians.

In 1861 Congress approved a bill to establish Colorado territory and Colonel William Gilpin, a hero of the Mexican war, was appointed governor. As a result more settlers, railroad builders and stagecoach operators began to flood into this underdeveloped land. The plains Indians who were already there, Arapaho, Comanche, Cheyenne and Kiowa, dismayed at this additional intrusion, went on the warpath and a bloodbath followed. Attitudes to the Indians differed. General Sherman said, "The more we can kill this year, the less will have to be killed in the next war, for the more I see of these Indians the more convinced I am that they all have to be killed or maintained as a species of paupers. Their attempts at civilization are simply ridiculous". The bloody uprisings were finally put down in 1865 by Federal troops released for frontier duty at the end of the Civil War, but the losses on both sides were extremely heavy.

Colorado became the 38th State of America in 1876, one hundred years after the signing of the Declaration of Independence, earning the nickname the 'Centennial State'. Today mining is still important, (90% of the world's supply of molybdenum is extracted at Climax) but so too is farming. Tourism is another vital source of income, with visitors arriving from all over the world, eager to enjoy Colorado's magnificent scenery, towering mountains, crystal clear lakes and rich forests, excellent sporting facilities and above all the freedom to breath unpolluted air and wander for miles without seeing another soul.

Beautiful Bear Creek in Colorado's Rocky Mountain National Park is shown *left,* and *above left* the Big Thompson River, whilst *overleaf* is pictured magnificent Bear Lake.

The beaver *below* makes his home amid the tranquil scenery of Beaver Ponds, in Hidden Valley *above,* and the chipmunk *right* and ground squirrel *far right* are two of the Park's most charming residents.

Isolated in the Roosevelt National Forest stands the Peaceful Valley Memorial Chapel *above*.

Shrouded in mist, Long's Peak, towering 14,255 ft high, dominates the skyline over Trail Ridge Road *above left*, whilst *below left* Highway 6 snakes its way through Loveland Pass and the Continental Divide.

Picturesque lakes stud the Park's landscape; Nymph Lake, dammed by sun-bleached tree trunks *top right;* Sprague Lake *centre right* and Dream Lake, seen *below right* with Hallett Peak and Flat Top Mountain, and *below*, with floating deadwood.

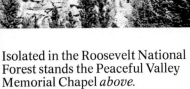

Denver the capital of Colorado, known as the 'Mile High City' is the commercial and cultural centre of the Rocky Mountain area. Set in landscaped grounds the city's Civic Center can be seen *above left* photographed from the State Capitol, and *above* the skyline pattern of Downtown Denver.

Situated on 17th and Broadway is the famous Brown Palace Hotel *left* and *below* the Molly Brown House, a picturesque Victorian house on Pennsylvania Street.

The Capitol building *overleaf*, was built between 1887 and 1895 and its distinctive 272ft. dome *right* is gilded in gold-leaf.

One of Denver's attractive suburbs, Golden, is shown *above* with the modern Coors Brewery dominating the landscape.

The magnificent 10,000 seat outdoor amphitheatre *left* is an outstanding feature of the Red Rocks Park and, with its craggy promontories *below* is one of Denver's most scenic attractions.

The Denver City Park Zoo houses a fine collection of animals from all over the world including the green iguanas, Bactrian camels, grey rhea, coyote, white naped crane and Aldabra tortoise illustrated *right*.

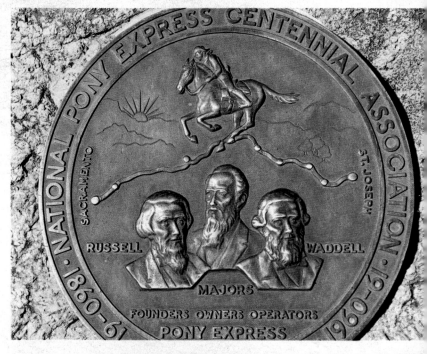

The Lace House *above left,* in Black Hawk, is typical of the architectural style of the 1860's, with its intricately carved bargeboard or 'gingerboard' trimming, whilst *below left* Black Hawk's Crook Palace claims to be the oldest bar in Colorado.

Reminiscent of a film set from a western movie are the pretty buildings shown *top, above, below and bottom right.*

At the top of Lookout Mountain, overlooking Denver, is the grave of W.F. Cody *top right,* where lies the body of the county's famous 'Buffalo Bill', and illustrated *centre right* is the Centennial Plaque of the Pony Express.

Central City *overleaf,* in the "Little Kingdom of Gilpin", is an old mining town established during the boom of the 1800's.

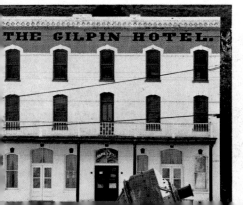

THE GOLDEN KEY
LODGING
& NEST IN FOOD & DRINKS
ENTRANCE
105
GOLDEN KEY · CENTRAL CITY

MISTER
YELLOW BELLOWS
PHOTOGRAPHER

GLORY HOL
TAVERN

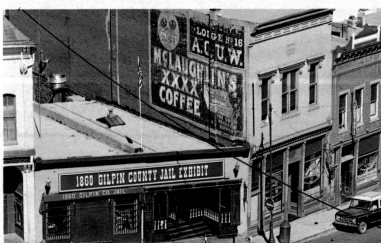

LOIGE No 18
A.C.U.W.
McLAUGHLIN'S
XXXX
COFFEE

1860 GILPIN COUNTY JAIL EXHIBIT
1860 GILPIN CO. JAIL

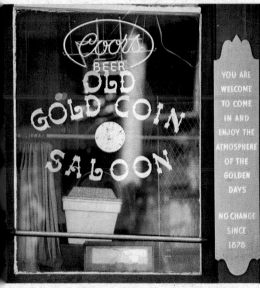

Coors
BEER
OLD
GOLD COIN
SALOON

YOU ARE
WELCOME
TO COME
IN AND
ENJOY THE
ATMOSPHERE
OF THE
GOLDEN
DAYS

NO CHANGE
SINCE
1878

BUFFALO
BILL
DRANK

TOL

GARTER

GILDED GARTER
CENTRAL CITY COLO. DIST. 8490
FAMILY GROUPS WELCOME

CITY HALL.

106
CLOSED

ROCK & LITE
SOME OLD / SOME NEW

I NEED YOU
FIGHT AGAINST
MUSCULAR DYSTROPHY

Once the first gold had been panned from the stream beds, during the discovery of the mid-1880's, the search for gold began in the mountains and thousands of hopeful prospectors poured into the district, but by the end of the century the mountains were deserted except for a few permanent mining towns.

Recalling those days of a by-gone era, when prospectors would throng the town with their pockets filled with hard-earned gold-dust, are the colourful façades of Central City's buildings *left and below,* most of which date back to Victorian times.

Preserved in Central City's famous Teller House are the finely burnished desk *above right,* and *centre right* the 'Face on the Barroom Floor" which was painted by the Denver artist Herndon Davis, in 1936, and inspired by H. Antoine D'Arcy's renowned ballad.

Amongst the many mines to be found in the area are the Coeur de Alene *above* and the Boodle *below right.*

The rugged canyon wilderness of
Dinosaur National Monument provides a
wealth of spectacular scenery in an area
rich in natural beauty. The Monument
derives its name from a deposit of fossil
bones in the south-west corner, excavated
from the river sediment in the 140-million-
year-old Morrison Formation, revealing
the petrified bones of turtles, crocodiles
and fourteen species of dinosaurs.
From Harper's Corner Trail magnificent
views of the canyon country can be seen
such as Round Top Mountain *top left*,
Green River with the Mitten Park Fault
left and the Canyon of Lodore *above*. Pool
Creek with the treeless Round Top
Mountain rising into the background is
shown *centre left* and the fertile region of
Steamboat Springs surrounding the Yampa
River *right*.
Threading its way like a silver snake
through majestic tree-studded mountains
is the Green River *overleaf;* icy and remote
in the blue morning air *left* and serenely
beautiful in the golden glow of the setting
sun *right*.

Aspen, cottonwoods, firs and pine trees
are a familiar part of the Colorado
landscape and particularly lovely when
tinged by Autumn hues as at Quartz
Creek, near Parlin *right*, whilst *above*,
against a stunning backdrop of trees,
cattle graze near Doyleville in
Gunnison County.

The spectacular Rio Grande River
flows over 18,000 miles before reaching
the Gulf of Mexico and courses its way
through a wealth of magnificent
scenery. The river can be seen near
South Fork *top left and centre left* and
in the rugged Creede area *bottom left*.

The swirling waters of the Cimarron
River, bordered by russet-leaved trees
are shown *below and overleaf*.

Breathtaking Monarch Pass *left*, at 11,312 feet, forms the Continental Divide between the Atlantic and the Pacific watershed, and from the Pass can be seen the magnificent vista of Tomichi Creek *above*.

The wide, rolling plains of Gunnison County *right* provide pasture for horses and in the background the thickly-forested, undulating mountains rise to meet the darkening sky.

The fast-flowing Crystal River *overleaf*, near the town of Marble, winds its way through the verdant splendour of the Gunnison National Forests.

MONARCH PASS
Elevation 11,312 feet

CONTINENTAL DIVIDE
PACIFIC   ATLANTIC

The beautiful Blue Mesa Reservoir shimmers in the Curecanti National Recreation Area *left and above left*, whilst *below* the peaks of Sheep and White Horse Mountains are reflected in the still waters of Island Lake, near Marble.

The massive pinnacles of Mt. Antero, seen from the top of Monarch Pass, are shown *bottom left*, and *above*, Slumgullion Pass near Lake City.

The Black Canyon of the Gunnison *right* derives its name from its sombre countenance, as little sunlight penetrates the deep and narrow gorge.

In Autumn, the leaves of the silver-barked aspen trees *overleaf*, flood the landscape with rich golden tones.

Colorado's Air Force Academy Cadet Chapel *above and below* soars 150 feet towards the sky, its seventeen spires glinting in the sunlight. Designed to meet the spiritual needs of cadets, seen during the lunch-time parade *right*, the glass, aluminium and steel structure contains a separate chapel for each of the major religious faiths; Protestant, Catholic and Jewish and, in addition, a special meeting-room for members of other faiths. The Protestant nave *left* is sited on the upper level with the remaining chapels and meeting-room located beneath it.

The Garden of the Gods Park, within the famous summer resort of Colorado Springs, contains the unusual monolithic sandstone structures shown *left and above left*.

Forming a magnificent backdrop to the spectacular Royal Gorge in the Pikes Peak region *right*, which is spanned by the world's highest suspension bridge, are the Sangre de Cristo Mountains, at the base of which is the densely-forested area *below right*.

The painting of Kit Carson *above* commemorates the efforts of this loyal colonel who successfully negotiated for peace with the Ute Indians at Fort Garland during 1866.

Symbol of the U.S.A. is the bald-headed eagle *above* at the Cheyenne Mountain Zoo.

Storm clouds gather over the San Luis Valley *left*.

Nestling at the base of Pikes Peak is Colorado Springs *above*, known as the 'Sunshine City' because of its delightful climate. In the foreground can be seen the Broadmoor Hotel complex, a self-contained resort.

High on the slopes of Cheyenne Mountain is the Will Rogers Shrine of the Sun *left and below*, an imposing fortress-tower constructed of local grey-pink granite and dedicated to the memory of the famous humorist.

The lovely Abbey School Order of Saint Benedict *right* is located in Canon City.

Originally a thriving silver mining centre, Georgetown, 'The Silver Queen of the Rockies' contains a rich heritage of carefully preserved Victorian buildings such as the picturesque Maxwell House *right* and the Bowman/White House *above left*.

The Hotel de Paris retains much of its original furnishings and was purchased by the Colonial Dames, in 1954, in order to preserve the building as a museum. The dining-room is shown *above* and the kitchen, with its antique stove and accessories *below*.

The famous Georgetown Loop Railroad *below left*, originally opened in 1884, connects the towns of Georgetown and Silver Plume.

Spread like a vast green/gold sea, the hills around Ashcroft, near Aspen, *above and left* flood the landscape with their vibrant hues. Tall aspen trees, near Aspen, are shown *below*, the autumnal lane at Dillon *above right* and the thickly forested banks of Maroon Creek *right*.

Majestic Maroon Lake *overleaf* is Colorado's most famous lake.

Aspen, in Pitkin County, was founded by prospectors in 1878 and with the discovery of silver became a prosperous mining community, with a population of 15,000 by 1887. In the early 1890's, however, the dramatic drop in silver prices saw the decline of the city and it was not until the 1930's that Aspen once again flourished – to become a cultural and recreational centre for skiing and winter sports.

The city can be seen *above* in early Autumn before the first snow falls, to cover the highland's fifty miles of ski terrain. *Far left* is the Chapel of the Prince of Peace and *left* one of Aspen's picturesque houses.

The old ghost town of Ashcroft is featured *right* showing the deserted cabins and equipment which have been preserved by the Aspen Historical Society as a reminder of the mining heritage.

Silver was first discovered in Ashcroft in 1879 and the booming township, established in 1880, was originally known as Castle Forks, renamed Chloride and finally Ashcroft. By 1900 the town had been abandoned and lay derelict until its acquisition by a group of skiing enthusiasts in 1937, and became, during the First World War, the early training area for the 10th Mountain Ski Troops. The pioneering efforts of Ted Ryan finally brought into being the cross-country ski-complex which he deeded to the Forest Service in 1951.

The fabulous ski centre of Steamboat is sited in Steamboat Springs, Colorado and offers 53 trails as well as gladed tree areas and with its 614 acres of skiable terrain promises fun and excitement for all grades of skiers. Experienced instructors are always available to provide expert tuition so that even beginners can enjoy the thrill of cross-country skiing in this winter-wonderland.

The mountain at Steamboat has a vertical drop of 3,600 feet, the second longest in Colorado, and features fifteen lifts, including a 90-car gondola.

Popular sleigh rides *above right* are also available and include rides up the mountainside where guests can enjoy dinner in one of the heated tents.

On the upper runs thickly encrusted trees *above left* stand watch over the skiers as they glide their way over the powdery snow.

This popular resort also offers ski-jumping at the Howelsen Hill Ski Jump Complex, ice-skating and swimming in the heated hot springs pools at the excellent lodging facilities.

Surrounded by magnificent mountain peaks, Ouray *top right,* known as the 'Opal of the Mountains', derives its name from the famous Ute Indian, Chief Ouray, one of America's most noted peace negotiators. This old mining town, with its hot springs fed pool, was once sacred ground to the Indians and became a flourishing mining centre after the discovery of a rich silver lode in 1875.

Within the majestic San Juan Range is Red Mountain *centre right,* close to the Million Dollar Highway, an outstanding engineering accomplishment, originally built by the Pathfinder Otto Mears, and which runs through some of the country's most breathtaking alpine scenery.

Reminiscent of the dusty mining era is the Fort Smith Saloon in Ridgeway *above* and *below* is shown the Impson Bros. garage, near Pacerville, on Highway 62.

Beautiful Trout Lake *right* is located between Dolores and Telluride, its shores thickly encrusted by forested trees.

The dilapidated Deadhorse Mill *left* teeters on its rocky bank in the Crystal River area.

Nestling high in the San Juan Mountains of Southwestern Colorado, close to the head of a beautiful glacial valley, is Telluride *above*, a popular resort community which still retains the colourful character of its early mining origins with its cluster of wooden houses *left*, tinker's house *above left* and Opera House *centre left*. Still an important mining centre in the state, the town owes its name to a type of silver and gold ore found in the presence of tellurium, called 'Telluride ores'. The large, old mines, such as the Liberty Bell, Smuggler and Tomboy, helped to increase the town's prosperity and supported a population of almost 5,000 in its hey-day, with numerous gaming saloons, bars and bordellos. Today the town is becoming increasingly popular as a winter ski area, the magnificent mountain range providing valuable skiing terrain when covered by snow.

The rugged grandeur of Mt. Sneffels rising 14,143 feet into the blue horizon is shown *right*, its slopes thickly carpeted with forests of conifers.

The numerous ghost towns to be found in Colorado's old prospecting districts are poignant reminders of times long past when eager searchers for gold and silver poured into the mountains in the hope of making their fortunes.

By using the high and spectacular jeep trails *below* visitors can explore the ramshackle remains of the once thriving communities of Animas Forks, near Silverton *above and above left*, Tomboy on the Imogen Pass *left* and Alta, near Telluride *below left*.

Deserted and forlorn, the old wooden buildings of Sneffels, near Ouray *right* are set against the lonely mountains, studded with dark green conifers, the silence broken only by the gentle lapping of a mountain stream.

Once a booming mining town in the midst of the San Juan Mountains, Silverton *below*, set in a beautiful mountain park, is today a major tourist attraction bringing passengers from Durango along the route established by the Denver and Rio Grande Western Railroad, in 1882.

Engine 478 *above* steams along the narrow gauge track towards Silverton's station shown *below right*, whilst the somewhat macabre reminder of the harsh life known to the early prospectors is displayed outside one of Silverton's carefully preserved buildings *right*.

The rainbow *left* falls softly over the San Juan Mountains where long ago many searched for their 'pot of gold'.

Within Monument Canyon *above* the massive wind-carved rock formations *left* dominate the terrain of this wild and rugged area, where towering cliffs such as those of Rim Rock *top left* rise steeply in the crystal air. The tunnel *below* is carved through the rock face on Rim Drive and *bottom left* is shown the majestic Independence Monument with the Book Cliff Mountains overlooking the rolling plains beyond.

A multitude of pre-historic ruins can be found in the fascinating Mesa Verde National Park which rises high above the Mancos Valley. Created by the early Pueblo Indians, the highly-developed cliff dwellings of Cliff Palace *right*, occupy a large cave in the precipitous wall of one of the Mesa Verde's twenty-eight canyons.

Horses quietly graze beneath tier upon tier of green aspens *overleaf*.